WINDS of DOCTRINE

DOCTRINE

The Theology of Barth, Brunner, Bonhoeffer, Bultmann, Niebuhr, Tillich

Addison H. Leitch

FLEMING H. REVELL COMPANY
WESTWOOD · NEW JERSEY

Except for those Scripture passages otherwise identified, the Scripture quotations in this book are from the *King James Version of the Bible.*

Scripture quotations identified as RSV are from the *Revised Standard Version of the Bible.*

*To "Grandpa" John Heslip, who
taught me more than he
realized, which I am increasingly
realizing myself.*

PREFACE

Karl Barth once referred to himself as a "bird in flight." He was trying to instruct those who would insist on calling Barth a "Barthian." He did not want himself classified in a fixed position, and, I suppose, to that extent he was "Barthian," whether he wanted to be or not.

My sympathies are with him as I present this little volume. It represents, in very brief form, what one man is able to see at this particular point in the history of theology, and particularly in the mass impact of modern theology.

For several years now, the present material has been used in one way or another in seminaries, in college classes, and in lay institutes. Thanks to Dr. John Huffman and the Winona School of Theology, I was given an opportunity to organize and present this material as five lectures under the G. Campbell Morgan Lectureship. The audience was made up basically of the faculty and students of the summer school of Fuller Theological Seminary, which at that time was joined with the Winona School of Theology. There were, in addition, other people in attendance from the various conferences at Winona Lake. The reception given these lectures was warm and encouraging; by publishing them, my hope is that they will reach a wider public, who will also find them of value.

I am very much indebted personally to Dr. John Huffman and to the administration of Tarkio College, which gave me the opportunity to prepare and present these lectures.

ADDISON H. LEITCH

Tarkio, Missouri

CONTENTS

1

Intellectual Beginnings

IN THE HISTORY of thought, the continuity and interdependence of ideas make it almost impossible to determine the exact time when any particular strand of thought has had its inception. For any given idea, it is usually possible to find beginnings as far back as the writings of Aristotle or Plato or even the pre-Socratics. To start there creates an impossible assignment, and to start at any later point in history is, in the nature of the case, a wholly arbitrary decision.

Especially in theology we have to be arbitrary, because we are perfectly aware that when Christianity broke into the mainstream of Western thought, it could do so only by adjusting to the vocabulary and thought modes of that day. Our creeds and confessional statements could be made known to the world at large only because the newness of Christianity was subjected to contemporary language, and so to contemporary thought, for definition and understanding. When, therefore, we look for the beginnings of modern theology, we accept arbitrary decisions involved by necessity in our choice of a starting point. For the present purposes, I have chosen a relatively late starting point, just for the sake of getting started, in the contributions of Kant, Schleiermacher, and Hegel, with some notice in passing of Ritschl. These men have been chosen primarily because they gather together the strands of Western thought which precede them, and give definition and thrust to the thought movements which follow them. They are watershed thinkers—in modern theology, their contributions are basic in the structure of modern thought.

Immanuel Kant was, as he admitted, awakened "from his dogmatic slumbers" by a recognition of the skepticism into which the thinking of men like Hume had finally brought philosophy. To start with, Locke had set for himself some definition of the extent and limitations of human thinking in his "Essay Concerning Human Understanding." He believed that human understanding demands an external world of substance "out there," and an internal world of the person, or ego, "in here"; these two worlds are joined by what we call our "sensations." The outside world makes itself known to the inside world through sense experiences, and these sense experiences are channeled into our inner life by way of the five senses. This description is, of course, an oversimplification of a great and pioneering work of a man of stubborn as well as subtle mind, but the description nevertheless serves the purpose of making plain the "common sense" approach of Locke (the British philosophers are still self-conscious about their "common sense"; the great Sam Johnson was not above kicking a man in the shins to get him back to "the way things really are"), which accepts the plain facts that there is a world to be known and there are knowers, and there are sensations in between. These facts are perfectly evident to any "right thinking" person.

"Not so," said Berkeley. That the ego receives and works over a flow of sensations, is evident enough. But can we really say anything for sure about the world "out there," except as the sensations give rise to experiences within. We know only what sensations of a certain sort do to our minds. Perhaps the external world has no real existence except in our minds, unless, as the good Bishop emphasized, the real existence is in the mind of God. Thus the structure of Locke—substance, sensation, ego—is altered by Berkeley, with substance quite possible, but not as objective knowledge.

Hume went all the way. He finally concluded that we can have no knowledge of the outside world of substance and no knowledge of the inside world of ego. All we can know is sensation, and since our senses are only five we can only know what five senses can tell us. Kant appreciated the viewpoint, but he thought that something more must be said about the reality of the ego, the reality of the external world, and the reality of God. For our purposes, Kant awoke from his "dogmatic slumbers" with a start!

Within the limitations of this study, we need to pursue only one of Kant's ideas—namely, that whereas Hume was probably right in pointing up our inability to objectify substance, ego, and God, he was wrong if he meant thereby to deny their existence or to deny them as useful and necessary realities. This is where Kant's difficult concept, the term "transcendental," is introduced. His "transcendentals" are substance, ego, and God; by the term "transcendental" he means that whereas we cannot prove the existence of nor define accurately the nature of ego, substance, and God, nevertheless we must accept the necessity of their existence. The ego, for example, is not an *object* of my own sensations, but it is the necessary *subject* of them. I cannot prove its existence objectively, but, unless I accept its existence, I cannot sensibly try to prove anything else. The ego is the accepted position *from which* my thinking moves, not the end position *toward which* my thinking moves. The ego is not a first "truth" so much as a first "thing," a presupposed a priori reality—not an object of proof, but subject of the whole proving process.

So with substance. Whatever is "out there" sets up rays, or waves, or corpuscles, or molecular activity, or whatever it is that "plays upon" our sense end-organs. Hume and Berkeley are right in saying that we only know what five senses will tell us about whatever substance may be, but the thing-in-itself, whatever its true nature, is a necessary reality to account for whatever it is that creates the sensations. Substance is not an object of knowledge, but it is a necessary reality if sensations are to exist at all.

God is a similar transcendental—not objective knowledge, but the necessary ground of the possibility of knowledge. Most simply, He is the Reason, or Organizing Reality, giving unity and sense to the complex interrelations between the inner and outer worlds of man's varied experiences.

By such reasoning, Kant answered the skepticism of Hume; he shifted the ground for reality from objective proof to the subjective necessity, from a posteriori to a priori foundations, from findings to foundations.

For modern theology, there derives from this discussion one residue—namely, that all the old, so-called proofs for the existence of God are suspect, and all the definitions of God or the listings of His attributes must be redone. Our knowledge of God becomes, not objective reality, but subjective necessity—a first truth. This is why Van Til in *The New Modernism,* a criticism basically of Barthianism, finds it necessary to attack Kant. If Kant is right, then creeds, confessionals, systematics, catechisms, and the like—the whole matrix of propositional theology—are undermined.

Schleiermacher makes his contribution to modern theology in the same general way, by shifting his emphasis in religion from objective reality to feeling. Here again, the emphasis is thrown on the subjective experience; it is emphasis again on the non-proven and nonprovable. We cannot reason ourselves to proofs of God, nor do we even have a faith supported by reasons. Religion is a feeling: as Bridgman, the Harvard physicist, has said about truth, it is "a feeling in my bones." Evidence is never conclusive; one can only "bet his life" that God exists. Increasingly one gets the feeling from this kind of feeling that if one were a master of Schleiermacher, even more than of Kant, he would have the clue to much of the religious thinking of our day.

It was Hegel who "organized" paradox for modern theology. We know from his philosophy how basic was his emphasis on the structure of things in terms of thesis and antithesis, with the resulting search for a new synthesis. Hegel, of course, generalized with this structure into the fields of history, ethics, politics, and other matters, but in theology he let loose the idea that it should be one of the expectancies of Christanity that truth will come to us paradoxically. We do not get clear answers to our questions, but discover the truth in some synthesis in which the paradox is not resolved, but settled or left to be settled on some higher level. The difficulty is, of course, that our synthesis, whatever it is, becomes the thesis for a new antithesis, and so on out. Thus we are engaged in endless conversations, dialogues, and dialetics. We find hanging around the edges of such thinking the possibilities of dialectical materialism, existentialism, and all kinds of relativisms.

Ritschl made his contribution by throwing the emphasis of religion on values. One might put it this way: it does not matter whether Jesus ever actually lived, so long as the idea of such a person was released into the consciousness of humanity. It was valuable that Christian teaching, from whatever source, became known to men. We must not be overly concerned with the historical Jesus or anything in the atonement which might be called a "transaction," nor do we need to concern ourselves with petty exactitudes in texts nor with the Scriptures, so long as the values abide.

As long ago as 1932, I heard a foreign missionary speak in such terms. Having given forty years of her life in sacrifice for her people, her flock, she was unclear about her convictions on Christ, but clear on Christian values, as if we could have the fruit without the root. This is the attitude of rice Christians; this is what makes everyone so happy about the success of the Peace Corps; this is the "escape clause" in public education—just no one will fight Christian "values." But, "What think ye of Christ"? This is the question which puts an entirely different light on things; this question makes the decisive difference. After all, we are happily advised, we are all going to the same hilltop by different roads; what does Christianity have that other religions don't have? Well, for one thing, Christianity has Christ!

In addition to men, there have been movements—movements not necessarily tied in with persons. Take, for example, the large and complex hypothesis under the general heading of "evolution." There is still some debate, even among biologists, over the definition of the term, and there is still some debate about the fact of, or the processes involved in, physiological evolution. We must recognize, however, that whatever may be said about biological evolution, a different kind of problem arises when we move from biological evolution to psychological evolution, or from psychology to religion. What happens to the whole idea of evolution when we make out of it a philosophy, an overreaching way of judging everything? How does it happen that most of the people talking about Darwin have never read Darwin? One of the happy discoveries we make in reading Darwin's writing is that he had the modesty of a true scientist. He qualifies what he has to say with such safeguards as "it would appear," or "one might be led to conclude," or "the facts seem to indicate." We must remember that this careful scientist was popularized by another person, named Huxley. What Darwin said by way of Huxley was made into a total philosophy by Spencer. The validity of this whole history of the launching of evolution on the world needs to be reworked by competent scholars. What we need to see now, however, is that growing out of the debate over biological evolution there emerged eventually a philosophy of evolution; this became a total way of looking at everything, from which men then concluded that there is a kind of built-in progress in the whole system of things. We have therefore learned to speak easily of the "evolution" of business, or the "evolution" of art, or the "evolution" of society, for which kinds of evolving there are no facts or figures whatsoever.

A repeated phenomenon in the teaching of philosophy on the college and seminary levels is the discovery of absolute and abysmal ignorance in the basic matters of both philosophy and theology. Even a basic vocabulary is missing in whole areas in which men have been doing profound and foundational thinking for centuries. This leads to wayward thinking regarding politics or aesthetics, metaphysics or epistemology, truth, and freedom. But if one just mentions the word "evolution," simply everyone smugly knows what he is talking about—the vocabulary is easy and the burden is light. This can mean only one thing:

evolution has become a climate of opinion, an atmosphere for thought. And this is its own danger: unproved itself, it becomes the foundation for other "proofs."

It is my opinion that the acceptance of what Nels Ferré calls the "mystique" of evolution was perhaps a prime mover in another phenomenon of the last century: what I would call "the radical criticism of the Bible." When evolution is applied to religion, and we talk easily about that kind of progression, it is assumed that religion has moved up from animism, to polytheism, to pantheism, to monotheism. It is then easy to assume that since monotheism comes last in the evolutionary process, it cannot appear first in Biblical history. It is not difficult to accept monotheism in Isaiah; but if evolution controls our thinking, we cannot allow monotheism as early as Genesis. We are assured, therefore, that monotheism in the early chapters of the Bible must have been added by later editors or redactors for their own subtle purposes. Now we are off and running on the whole complex of EJPD* so that even though discrepancies can be shown in the whole Graf-Wellhausen approach, the idea is tenaciously held that something like the layers of manuscripts back of the Biblical text has to be true because the evolution of religion is, "scholars agree," no longer debatable. The idea that animism and polytheism might well be the disintegration of monotheism rather than the ancestors of monotheism, might have an equally good case made for it, but it appears that modern theologians have accepted "the assured findings" of radical Biblical criticism, which may well have been rooted and grounded in the inaccurate findings of believers in the evolution of monotheism.

Schmidt's theory of "the high gods," on the contrary, the theory that monotheism came first and is still the backdrop for all the polytheisms front-stage, is a stubborn viewpoint that has been around for a long time and is getting increasing acceptance. Yet

* These letters stand for the various assumed ancient manuscripts back of the Bible. E = Elohim, J = Jahweh, P = Priestly, D = Deuteronomic. E and J stand for the titles for God characterizing certain sections of Old Testament records.

a man of my acquaintance, after nineteen years in the Cameroons, with a mastery of native tongues and customs, barely achieved his doctorate in an eastern university because of his insistence, based on his experience and insight, over against his examiners' "assured findings" of scholarship (two of his examiners had never even been to any part of Africa), that monotheism, in even the most degenerate tribes, is first in order and basic to all other religious thinking.

Our view of evolution will condition our view of man. Can science have a doctrine of man? Maybe science cannot have a doctrine of man. It is the method of science to abstract, to bring bits and pieces of the whole under rigid controls for the sake of sharp, narrow data. If the disciplines of psychology and sociology are to be sciences, it should be recognized that a narrow rather than a full view of man must be their concern. It is in literature —plays, poetry, novels—that we must look for representation of the whole man, and it can be hoped that literature in our day shall in no wise be emasculated by a psychology trying to be a science, by a view of man which is clinical, endlessly analytic, and dead—a corpse in a medical school, instead of a person in a doctor's office. Significantly, not very nice things are being said about the whole man in literature; his progress is not so evident as evolutionists might hope; there are some built-in flaws, some twists in the very grain of life.

Beginning with Kierkegaard and running through to Camus and Tennessee Williams by way of Dostoevsky and Sartre, the word on man is harshly pessimistic. Kierkegaard's approach was not acceptable in his day (but has begun to make sense in our day), for he was a writer who, in the face of the "mystique" of evolution, still recognized the exceeding sinfulness of sin, its radical nature demanding a radical cure. Dostoevsky, by means of his novels, also opposed the trend of happy optimism. Today in such men as Sartre, Camus, and Williams, where the religious dimension has been discounted entirely, we at least have a modern and sophisticated acceptance of the radical nature of sin. Having no hope for mankind, they at least are forced to recog-

nize mankind's deep need and unanswerable predicament. The
have no gospel, but, as Oppenheimer, the great physicist, ha
stated it for scientists, they have in some sense "known sin."

Thus, thinking about evolution leads our minds in two diverse
directions. In the easy, noncritical assumptions regarding evolution, there is some foundation for similar easy assumptions about
the critical tampering with the Bible, and at the same time there
are strong, counter literary criticisms, especially in the study of
modern man, which make any assumptions regarding the hopeful
prospects for man very dubious indeed. Freud is a good example
of a man of great repute and wide acceptance who was both a
literary figure and a psychologist as scientific as a psychologist can
be. Speaking for himself, his great host of disciples, and even his
great host of pseudodisciples, speaking indeed for that which is
most widely agreed upon in modern psychology and psychiatry,
what is he saying to us? What are modern psychology and psychiatry saying to us? The word is out now and it is simple—"Out of
the heart are the issues of life." Also, "As a man thinketh in his
heart, so is he." But the heart is not good; something is wrong in
the deeps. The wellsprings of life are polluted. The exceeding
sinfulness of sin is radical, "of the root," and demands radical
treatment.

Another conditioner of theology has been the physical sciences.
It has been said that the two characteristics of modern physics are
probability and relativity. Both concepts make their contribution
to modern theology. Nothing is final, nothing is "for sure" or
"for keeps." So much depends on the stance and viewpoint of the
observer. There are physicists who say that even to look at a
thing changes the object while it is under observation. With their
nonobjective, paradoxical, existential, and irrational aspects,
physics and theology have common bonds.

It is interesting to wonder which came first—has theology created the intellectual atmosphere of hesitation, or is theology
conditioned by that atmosphere. For what is common to physics
and theology, is common wherever one may turn: the relativisms
in an education without absolutes; equity as against law in juris-

prudence; freedom from norms in the arts; and when one would insist on a position in ethics he is told, "Don't be a legalist!"

If our judgment in these matters has been correct, then modern theology has been building on a great many ideas, some more or less assured, some highly debatable, which have been carried over from the nineteenth into the second half of the twentieth century. We have attempted to characterize these ideas according to certain well-known philosophers and certain well-known men and movements in the ongoing tradition of western thought. We recognize the sources from which these ideas have arisen. We recognize, also, that for most theologians these concepts have become more or less normative. In a brief recapitulation, these ideas stand:

1. Serious questions have been raised regarding objective knowledge. "Absolute objectivity," said Brunner, "is absolute nonsense." The physicist Bridgman insists that objective knowledge depends on the subject, on the stance of the observer.
2. The acceptance of this idea leads us to an emphasis on the subjective. An emphasis on the subjective, especially how one himself feels, allows for considerable nonrational experience as support for religion. This opens the door to everything related to existentialism. How one *really* feels about something may determine for him in a given situation, in a given moment of existence, what he *really* believes his course of action ought to be.
3. The playing down of the objective and the playing up of the subjective permit all kinds of relative judgments. There is no place for propositional or systematic theology in the classic or orthodox sense. Particularly in ethical applications of theology, legalisms and moralisms are highly suspect. Starting with a wobbling doctrine, we compound our error by a wobbling ethic.
4. After a century of emphasis on evolution the terminology

and atmosphere remain, and no one concerned for his scholarly reputation would dare to question that. Yet the happy optimism that "day by day in every way we are getting better and better" has been badly mauled.

5. Our day is marked, not only in theology, but in secular disciplines by a new acceptance of the radical nature of sin. This is all to the good. Sin is no longer an evolutionary overhang. It is not to be commended as "modern" or "sophisticated," but it is built into the condition of man, it is alive in the marrow of a man. Freud, Kierkegaard, Camus, and such writers have assured us that a man's heart is exceedingly and subtly wicked. This is not to say that they have accepted any suggestions equally radical for man's redemption. Indeed, the fact of the matter is that there is now a deep pessimism abroad regarding man, but strangely interlocked with a continuing belief in *evolution in some sense*. This strange dichotomy awaits more scholarly work.

6. The critical apparatus for the study of the Scriptures is widely accepted in theological circles. The assumptions in the teaching of most seminaries of most denominations start with the easy acceptance of the old Graf-Wellhausen structures, and it is probably the most widely accepted theory of the thinking of the last 100 years in Biblical scholarship. In spite of the fact that serious questions have been raised against the whole higher critical approach to the Scriptures, it is difficult to find either a seminary or a scholarly journal which is not committed to such views.

In the chapters which follow, it will be evident how these various ideas affected the thinking of Barth, Bultmann, Tillich, and others; sometimes these nineteenth-century views dominate. It should be equally evident as we proceed that stringent criticisms are called for. There is also need for some kind of an evaluation of the orthodox counter-movement and some judgment of its strength.

Karl Barth

2

IT HAS BEEN said, and I think rightly, that the test of an expert in any field is whether one can speak authoritatively in that field without reference to that man. It has become impossible in our day to touch any theme in theology with any seriousness without reference pro or con to Karl Barth. As his *Dogmatik* has been slowly moving over to English, the theological world is becoming increasingly aware of the massiveness as well as the originality of this man's productivity. How can one put his finger at the center of Barth's theology; how can one find the starting point for that theological system which has become known as "the Barthian movement"?

For the present purposes, I find it useful to begin with Barth's interpretation of the Scriptures. His book *The Word of God and the Word of Man*, although perhaps not his greatest, is the clearest clue, in my opinion, to everything else that he has done.

We hear it said that Barth's viewpoint on Scripture began to formulate when, as a young man in his first pastorate, he raised a serious question with himself—a question which perhaps young pastors ought not to raise with themselves, for it is "nought for their comfort." Barth was the product of the normal, liberal teaching in the German universities of his day, and he had been much impressed by Harnack and Hermann. He had been conditioned by the radical, higher criticism of German rationalism, and he knew that the Bible from which he preached was subject to all kinds of criticism, not only with regard to the specific manuscripts, with their different versions and translations, but in the deeper questions of form criticism and the like. It was incumbent on him on any given Sabbath morning, nevertheless, to preach from the Bible. His question to himself, therefore, was: "What happens when I preach?" What exactly was he doing; what was going on; or, more to the point, what was supposed to be going on? Could it be said that he was preaching the word of God from the Word of God? Was he in any sense using the "words of God?" In working on such questions, he came to his central doctrine of the "Word."

He recognized, as we all do, that there was a time in the history of the Scriptures when it could be said that the material was in some sense officially organized into the official and accepted document. This need not have been, but could have been, what the fundamentalist would call the "divine originals." But them we no longer have.

Most Old Testament scholars agree that there were about twenty-two documents as Old Testament sources. The "Book of Jasher" referred to in the account of the long day in Joshua is a clear case in point. The Old Testament prophets must have had some official judgment passed sometime on the final shuffling of their various sheets of material; the cavalier fashion in which Jeremiah and Baruch, not to mention the gentlemen of the opposition, treated Jeremiah's writings, is frightening. Luke reflects in his Gospel preface that many other attempted gospels must have been circulating in the first century. Ur-Mark, Q, *ta loggia,* and the like, are attempts to capture critically what these New Testament sources might have been. There seems to have been a grand carelessness in sending Paul's writings about—could there have been four letters to the Corinthians for example? The corpus of Paul's basic writings is, as we now have it, the end-product of occasional letters, carried here and there inside somebody's shirt.

There had to be a time sometime, however, when it could be said of any Biblical manuscript: "It stands written." From this "original" there then arose codices, translations, versions, and paraphrases, sometimes produced by a group of scholars, sometimes the brilliant efforts of individual men. Since we do not have the divine originals, and since even an amateur linguist is aware of the impossiblities of literal translations even if we had the originals, what do we mean when we talk about the "Word of God" or, more narrowly, the "words of God"? Unless we have the original words or unless the translations into over 1,000 languages can convey the original words, in what sense can we say that we actually have the Word of God? So much for the Bible in our hands.

This still leaves the question of the necessity of the Words being preached. If the Bible is what God has to say to man, why does the preacher have to say anything at all? Let the Bible speak its own message. Would it not be a good scheme, for example, to have a man with a very well trained voice record the whole of Scripture and then have the recording played from time to time while people listened to the Bible instead of listening to somebody preach *about* the Bible or from the Bible? Why do we need another witness?

As Barth wrestled with this problem, and I think it is worth our own serious thinking, he recognized that in the providence of God there is somehow a necessity for the preacher. Something else has to happen in and around or above and beyond the recorded words. Look at the experiences of Peter and Cornelius. Peter and Cornelius each had his own vision directly from God, and yet each man's vision was incomplete. There was the necessity apparently for Peter after *his* vision to speak personally to Cornelius after *his* vision, before the whole message of God was complete. Cornelius needed God's word from Peter, and I expect that Peter needed to be a channel for God's word for his own personal instruction and growth. A man "called" to preach is a man with a message to whom this Word of God has come; he feels the burden of communicating that Word to those about him. But every man called to preach will have his own message, too.

Warfield's illustration of the windows in a cathedral is helpful in explaining this. He developed it as an illustration on inspiration and revelation. When the light of the sun (one is reminded of Plato's "parable of the cave" here) strikes the stained-glass windows of the cathedral, there is but one light, but there are widely varied windows through which the light moves. In like manner, the Word of God is diffused through an Amos or a Luke—the Word of God "as we find it in Amos," the Word of God "according to Luke." There is no hint of mechanical dictation here—full allowance is made for the person of the prophet, the integrity of the evangelist. But what Warfield is careful to point out is that the Creator, not only controls the light of the sun, but also has designed and colored the windows; He has been careful about the light, and meticulous in preparing the channels for His light. Jeremiah was being prepared from the time he was in his mother's womb.

The borrowing from Warfield here makes Barth clearer, by changing the example so that the light is from the Bible and the preacher is the window. Barth believed that the Word, coming into being as the message, is colored by the messenger. The messenger is also a creation in God's providence. But beyond this there is the wall of the cathedral catching the light, and at various seasons and at various times of the day the light through the various windows has its own existential effect in each different place where it falls. The great architect has the grand design, for he understands light and builds for proper lighting. It is always an interesting assignment in seminary classes to see how every member of a class comes up with a different treatment of the same passage of Scripture. In such an exercise, what has happened to the divine "original?"

Barth came to the conclusion that the "Word of God" is not a question *finally*, although it may be a question *primarily* of the words of Scripture. The Word of God is involved in a whole process, beginning with the original manuscripts and ending with action—*i.e.*, those who hear the preaching become the "epistles known and read of all men." In all this there is an understanding of Christ as the Living Word, who nevertheless comes alive in the life of the hearer, the believer.

Even those who are most adamant in holding to the words of Scripture or the inerrancy of divine "originals" must also admit and accept Christ finally as the Living Word. What is His relationship to the "writings"? The clue is in the opening passage of the Gospel according to John and the opening verses of Hebrews. "In the beginning was the Word, and the Word was with God, and the Word was God" (JOHN 1:1). It is soon evident in John's treatment that the Word is Christ for ". . . the Word became flesh and dwelt among us . . . and we have beheld his glory . . ." (JOHN 1:14, RSV). In Hebrews we read: "In many and various ways God spoke of old to our fathers by the prophets; but in these last days he has spoken to us by a Son . . ." (HEBREWS 1:1,2, RSV). God had something to say to man, which He said "in many and various ways," but what He finally said to man He said in a Person, even Jesus Christ. But this same Christ, not only set forth the Living Word, He spoke *words* of final authority: ". . . to whom shall we go? thou hast the words of eternal life" (JOHN 6:68). Then came the writers of the Gospels and epistles "That which we have seen" . . . and ". . . handled, of the Word of life . . . declare we unto you, that ye also may have fellowship with us . . ." (I JOHN 1:1–3). Thus, both "Word" and "words" are reduced to a written message of "words." These "words" of Jesus the Word and of His "wonderful words of life" become the basis again of reading, preaching, and the life of the church, the Living Body of Christ. That Word, which was from the beginning with God, comes alive in us. This is again the magnificence of the whole story: Christ in us is finally the hope of glory; the church is the Body, of which He is the Head. Yet all of this is a continual and continuous process, creative of the evangel and constantly created by the evangel.

Something of this structure is what Barth arrived at: the preacher, like Barth in his pulpit, in a small town in Germany reads his German Bible, searches in the Hebrew and Greek, and consults the best of the commentaries in order to discover, not only what the words of his German Bible say, but what was understood in the ancient world and what was meant in the ancient world when these words first appeared. This is why he will work with every help available, not only languages, but manners and customs, and, if he is so minded, with "form criticism," demythologizing, anthropology, and archaeology. A man has his own preparation here, according to his integrity and the sensitivity and control of his imagination. Thus, preacher Barth brings to bear on a particular passage what he himself is— namely, such and such a young preacher, with such and such an education, and with such and such mature and amateur experiences. Why, in the providence of God, did he choose one particular passage for preaching instead of another? Why these illustrations instead of those? What, finally, will his own personality and speaking style do to all this that another man's couldn't or shouldn't? At the other end of this process are the hearers, a mixed bag of backgrounds, intellects, ages, conditions spiritual and intellectual. What each one "gets" out of all this will represent a wide variety of possibilities. What each one will do in terms of what he has heard will, in turn, be determined by almost endless variants.

It is easy from all this to grasp the length and breadth of the whole idea of existentialism during the thirty minutes of a sermon. Whatever is communicated will be determined by the moment of existence in which the preacher finds himself, and the moment of existence in which every member of his congregation finds himself.

What we must keep in mind is that in all this process, or in thinking of the Word as a dynamic process, Barth does not accept the criticism that there are no fixed points of reference. He holds fast to the canon of Scripture as the channel through which God's Word begins and he has, of course, a high opinion of the Holy Spirit. Assuming the wide variants in preachers and hearers, we need not thereby believe that the Spirit is arbitrary. Working "where and when and how He pleases" does not mean that the Spirit works any old way at all. Men as variables will be unified by one Spirit.

This is good Lutheran and Reformed theology, the theology

of Word-Spirit and Spirit-Word. The Spirit works only with the Word which the Spirit originally inspired; the Word is not the "letter that killeth" when it comes "alive" as the Spirit plays upon it. There are controls here for some of the wilder expressions today of those who are filled with the Spirit; there is instruction here for those who would be guided only by the "inner light." Our modern use and misuse of "love" as "the only absolute" may even be a new and interesting evasion of the boundaries of the Word; not so with Barth, for he believes that only the Spirit and the Word can tell us first what love really is, and how in our situation it must be brought to bear on life. Like the man who made the interesting discovery that he had been speaking a thing called "prose" all our life, more of us than will readily admit have been preaching like Barth all our lives. How do you really choose your text, get at your message, get at your people, preach to conviction and action. Is not your own prayer that God will rule and overrule, have His own way with His Word?

This is where Barth sees the opportunities of the Holy Spirit of God, who "takes of the things of Christ and shows them unto us." The "Word" of God and the "Spirit" of God unite in this whole process, and this is good Reformed theology. The Spirit works with the Word "when and where and how He pleases." If, in following Barth, we wish to speak of the "Word of God," it is this whole complex and process.

Certain terms characteristic of Barth need attention. The "Word of God," as Barth structures it, we have already explored. The idea of "paradox" (which Barth discovered from Hegel, Heidegger, Kierkegaard, and that whole tradition) arises when a man listening to the Word of God finds himself in a crucial decision on dead-center, where something can be said for both sides of a case. This shows up particularly when, under the impact of the sermon, we are called to action in ethical decisions. Then the Word of God can lead a man to a decision existentially which may not be the same decision of the man sitting next to him in the pew. Thus, Barthianism as a "crisis theology" has its meaning for each man—according to God's Word to him, he must in faith make his own "crisis" judgments.

In back of his acceptance of "paradox" and his emphasis on "crisis" is Barth's deep devotion to, and his deep concern for, "faith." In all the confusions and alarms of life, in all vital decisions in everyday's living, we can, we must, walk by faith. God calls us and speaks to us; we hear the Eternal Word breaking into our moment of time. There is place and time *now* for Christ to come alive in us and through us. As Milton expresses it in another context, one walks "as ever in my great Taskmaster's eye." This is good, for our line of recognition and obedience runs towards God and not towards man. "One step enough for me" as one walks under the Word. "Faith" now means the assurance that God covers our actions, redeems our times, picks up the loose ends. Having put our hand to the plow, we do not turn back. We understand something here of Luther, when he said to "sin boldly," for no man walks perfectly, but it is God nevertheless who can work in us for His good pleasure. Luther also said: "Here I stand, God help me. I can do no other." Thus, all our strivings cease. Resting in the Lord we find strength and peace. As John Oman suggests, the guidance of God does not mean that we shall face no storms; it does mean that we shall at last find harbor.

Barthianism, in addition to these general terms, also comes under the broader title of "neo-orthodoxy," a term which also makes its own good sense. In what way can we call Barthianism "orthodoxy"? In the first place, it is Bible-centered. This has always been a prime requisite of orthodoxy, and within his own lights Barth is orthodox at this point. Whatever it is that God is going to say to us, He will say it to us only by way of canonical Scripture. There is no pseudosophistication here about the inspiring impact of Milton or Shakespeare, as if their writings somehow were of equal validity with the Bible. There is no nonsense in Barth's beliefs that some other written word can be as authoritative.

The Barthian movement is also orthodox in its emphasis on sin. In the preceding chapter, we underlined the new emphasis today on the radical nature of sin. This Barth accepts. "Sin" in man is in the deeps, in man's essence, his nature. As a German

27

pastor after World War I (one can almost note the echoes here of *All Quiet on the Western Front*) and as a German professor, mostly during the frightfully revealing days of the Hitler regime, he would find this view of built-in human sin increasingly easy to believe.

His theology is also Christ-centered. It is my judgment that the truly magnificent portions of Barth's *Dogmatik* have to do with Redemption and the Redeemer. This is as it should be. The deep needs of man require deep therapy. Man needs the completed work of God Himself the mighty act in Christ. We are healing the hurt hardly with our jolly cures for deadly disease. A theology which is Bible-centered and Christ-centered does not deal lightly with the things of God and men. A mark of Barth's theology is that all of the old, easygoing treatments of God are dismissed. Whatever is meant by "the gentle Jesus, meek and mild," it does not mean a Jesus who could stomach the sight of a little one led to stumbling. Better for the one who led him to stumble that he be drowned in the depths of the sea. The look of Jesus—is it Heaven or Hell? Ask Peter, who went out into the night to weep—and to repent. No place of grace without that face.

Barth envisions God in His utter majesty and holiness, the One who is "wholly other." God initiates, God breaks in, God sustains, God fulfills, the promise is of God, not of man. For those of us who survived the predepression preaching in American churches, there is something deeply satisfying in the gritty grasp that Barth has on "wonder" and "light" and "holiness." Brunner may well critize this viewpoint in relation to natural theology; there is a God who draws near. Barth's concern and emphasis remain; any nearness is of God's initiative and control and purpose, and any natural theology which is only natural lacks the word of repentance and redemption. Barth's commentary on Romans smashed into European theology with a mighty message—the One with whom we have to do is God *Almighty*. He speaks His own word, and absolutely.

Why, then, is this *orthodoxy* called *neo?* Well, those who have come from the orthodox tradition of Hodge and Warfield and perhaps Machen, or have learned from Van Til or Henry or Carnell or Murray or Ramm, *know* that the *orthodoxy* of Barth is *neo*. We are not ready to accept his radical criticism of the Bible. When he will consider as allegory or legend that which we claim to be sober history, just so long as the "Word" comes through, we begin to see our differences. Also, followers of Barth are too ready to accept Biblical truth as paradox. Perhaps the easy acceptance of paradox is too quickly and too easily the evasion of truth instead of the way to truth. After all, when we learn to say that there are several ways of looking at ambiguous matters, we end up by saying that one way is as good as another.

We cannot evade, as neo-orthodoxy does, the necessity laid on us for the sharpest kind of definition of which we are capable in current and systematic theology. This is not to say that we know all the answers, but it is to say, as Aristotle discovered centuries ago, that both reason and language are useful tools for distinguishing "this" from "that." And this kind of distinction is what makes knowledge. I have heard it said too many times that the "virgin birth" is not important, and may just be a way of expressing a great truth, like the incarnation. Nevertheless, the word "virgin" is a clear enough word to all of us, and meanings are easily drawn from what this word conveys to us. When two of the four Gospels tell us of a "virgin birth," then we are faced with genuineness and authenticity of the sources; we must not, for whatever reasons, ruin language as a tool. Those who oppose sharp creedal statements sneer at a catechism which tries to define "God." Yet the definition is clear, even if it is not complete. Describing God as a "Spirit" certainly eliminates all idea that He is "matter." God "infinite" is not an explanation of "infinity," but makes it clear that He is not "finite," as we are. So one moves through all the words of definition. We all know that finite minds cannot enclose infinity, and we are aware of Kant's warning regarding our antimonies. Nevertheless, "He has written eternity in our hearts"—and we know about all kinds of things worth defining in the infinities and the eternities.

In an attempt to arrive at some kind of special wisdom in the refusing of sharp definitions in theology, many are being exceedingly foolish. Try the following exercise on any denomination and consider its relationship to its own creeds. What, for example, is a Presbyterian?—and I am not raising the question of the form of government, but of theological content. Either a Presbyterian is one who is loyal to the Westminster Confession or he is something else. If he is not loyal to that confession, in what way shall he be defined?* The answer to this is usually as follows: "Don't put us in a theological straitjacket; let's have no theological witch-hunting." This kind of response I consider to be an "out," rather than an answer. But suppose we accept the freedom from definition as a principle. After all, the important thing is to be a Christian, not a Presbyterian. Very well, a Protestant or a Romanist Christian? Will not the attitude that refuses to draw lines between Presbyterians and Baptists or between Protestants and Romanists eventually blur the distinctions between Christians and Buddhists or Moslems? It will, and it does. Or shall we just learn to love people? But then, does not Jesus define "love" for us in words and in living Word? And is this not a definition? If, as is so frequently suggested, we all get to the hilltop by different roads, doesn't this beg the whole question as to what we are looking for at the hilltop?

It is in this sense that we are willing to give due weight to the use of our reason in the support of our faith. We need not make our proofs for religion absolute, and yet they exist, as Gerstner has pointed out in the title and content of his fine apologetic, *Reasons for Faith*.

Barthianism is, therefore, neo-orthodox; we rejoice in its sturdy orthodoxy, as we shy away from the weaknesses of its novelties.

---

* What I say here could be applied to the Confession of 1967 in whatever form it takes or, for that matter, any confessional statement of any denomination.

3

Three Barthians: Brunner, Bonhoeffer, and Niebuhr

THE ADVICE IS generally given, and it is well taken, that one of the best ways to understand Barth is to read *H. Emil Brunner*. Brunner has a color and clarity to his style not often characteristic of the German theologians, which is certainly different from the straightforward, driving style of Barth. Brunner's early writing is his best. In the thirties he produced what I am sure were his greatest books, at least nothing since has surpassed them—*The Divine Imperative* and *The Mediator*. Both books are suffering from some neglect now. I have met seminary graduates who are unacquainted even with the titles, but, like many great books, they may have a season "underground" before being restored. *The Divine Imperative* will, in my opinion, become a classic in both sociology and religion, standing with Troeltsch's *Social Teaching of the Christian Churches*. Why these volumes, in a day of wars on poverty and battles on race, are not being studied is a mystery, or maybe a sign of the superficiality of approach to modern social problems.

Sir Edwin Hoskyns brought Barth's *Romans* into English at about the same time as Olive Wyon's translations of Brunner appeared. It is amazing how the two theologians, each with a remarkably fine mind, have been able to stay so close together in their thinking for almost forty years. Both men have breadth of spirit to match massiveness of mind, and their good hearts have managed to absorb many criticisms. The irenic spirit displayed by Brunner when he was being attacked while at Princeton is illustrative—he shook the dust off his shoes and went on. Barth has been more polemical—toward Brunner, toward Bultmann— and perhaps Brunner has been the peacemaker. Their long association remains remarkable. When one speaks of men and movements in the recent past, one may say, in general, that Barth and Brunner are almost inseparable.

Only one marked difference appeared between them, and this was over the question of "natural theology," Brunner supporting and Barth denying. Significantly, what appeared to be a complete rift has now largely disappeared because of adjustments in the thinking of both men, but primarily in the thinking of Karl Barth. Karl Barth's *Nein!* was a harsh piece of writing, an attack in which he tried to beat down Brunner's view.

Both Barth and Brunner consider themselves reformed theologians. Both of them believe that in some measure they are in the true tradition and the right interpretation of Luther and Calvin. In order to understand the division between Barth and Brunner, the movement of Calvin's thinking on the subject of natural theology is worth noting. Very briefly, Calvin's theology starts with the affirmation that theology is the "knowledge of God." "Our wisdom," he says as he begins his majestic *Institutes,* "in so far as it ought to be deemed true and solid wisdom, consists almost entirely of two parts: the knowledge of God and of ourselves." But he concludes vol. I, book I, chapter I, like this: "Though the knowledge of God and the knowledge of ourselves are bound together by a mutual tie, due arrangement requires that we treat of the former in the first place, and then descend to the latter." After discussing this knowledge in relation to other areas of knowledge, Calvin comes out strongly for natural theology—*i.e.,* "the heavens declare the glory of God," and there is "a light lighting every man coming into the world." Calvin's whole treatment of "the things of this world" in acceptance and in denial is a study in itself, and his acceptance of natural theology is quite inescapable. But simply to say this is not the end of the matter. It is typical of Calvin's theology that he gives completely with one hand and then takes away completely with the other, and in this way makes his own contribution to paradoxes in modern theology.

Those who have studied the writing on Calvin in recent decades know to what extent the central teaching, the clue, the essential thrust of Calvin, has been the theme of many scholarly studies. Popularly, the central characteristic of Calvin is "predestination." Others suggest "faith," or "grace," or the like. My preference is "the honor of God." How many times Calvin's approach to a theological theme is protective of that honor. This is why we find the peculiar emphasis we do in his treatment of natural theology. Calvin must insist that there can be no criticism of God; God has done everything an Almighty God can do. The world of nature reveals God to natural eyes: ". . . his invisible nature, namely, his eternal power and deity, has been clearly perceived. . . . So they are without excuse." But what Calvin gives, Calvin takes away.

Having argued the case for natural theology, he then points out that, whereas man *could know* God through the world of nature, man *does not know* God through the world of nature because his eyes are blinded by sin; his natural efforts, instead of reaching God, end up in idolatry—he worships the creature instead of the Creator. God, therefore, has been graciously pleased to supply us with a special revelation in Scripture. In this there are things to be known of God which would not be evident naturally in nature; since the problem of natural theology is "sin," the special revelation of the Bible sets forth what can now be called "saving knowledge"—namely, the revelation of redemption in the life and death of Christ, and the power of His resurrection. As Calvin would express it, the Scriptures are the "divine spectacles," bringing into focus what the world of nature without special revelation suggests to us out of focus, resulting eventually in confusion, the blind ending up leading the blind. Significantly, this special revelation does not become saving knowledge for all men, as is perfectly evident by the way many react neutrally or negatively to the story of salvation. At this point, the Holy Spirit of God must act upon the heart in a saving fashion. It is here that we must step manfully into the whole idea of "election," for it is evident that the Holy Spirit of God quite evidently uses the Scriptures in a saving fashion on some men and not on others, and it is only when a man has been thus saved that the whole world of natural theology opens up to him and begins to make sense: "behold I make all *things* new."

Both Brunner and Barth, therefore, can support themselves from Calvin, and they do—Brunner beginning as Calvin does, with the acceptance of natural theology; Barth, in typical fashion, throwing his emphasis on the basic necessity of the act of God to make all this saving knowledge meaningful. It is evident that they each have a good case, and, after the stubbornness of the argument, they both arrive more or less at Calvin's position. God is good enough to reveal Himself in nature to all men; we are bad enough not to "get it"; and He is gracious enough to provide another revelation through which, in the mystery and wisdom of His sovereign will, He can elect some to the way of salvation.

We are not now arguing the validity of this basic Calvinism. We are simply pointing out that Barth's stubborn emphasis is on the "wholly otherness" of God, and Brunner sits a little looser with the possibility of man's abilities, the marred but not obliterated image of God in man, by which his natural abilities have a rather wide range of possibilities. Barth has sympathy and empathy for Calvin on the side of election, whereas Brunner likes the way Calvin is not willing to minimize God's many good gifts. "This is my Father's world"; there are evidences of His presence constantly; the whole parabolic teaching of Jesus, where "The kingdom of God is like . . ."; the idea of the sacramental, where we have physical signs of spiritual realities; indeed, the incarnation itself, where the Word of God is revealed—these all lean toward Brunner's side of the argument. What has finally hap-

34

pened is that what is called the "new Barth"—that is, the later writings of Barth—have swung around in this direction. Neither Barth nor Brunner would be quite ready for the cry of many of our ecclesiastical tycoons that we are called to "listen to the world," a new slant arguing that, without the controls of Scripture and without the ongoing life of the church, the message and the messenger are out there somewhere among lost humanity. Not so, they would insist. The very opposite is true. It is not a matter of the church listening to the world—the world must listen to the church. The same Gospel comes in grace or in judgment; the good news cannot change, but the world must, or be damned.

This discussion on natural theology opens up as we see inviting and valuable vistas. To my mind, however, the greatest contribution of Emil Brunner to modern theology is in another direction—his treatment of the "image of God." There may be those who have discovered this idea elsewhere or for whom this is not such a commanding idea, but, for many of us, it has been, not only a revelation in itself, but a kind of open door toward many other possibilities.

The childish approach to the idea of the image of God is to believe that men look like God, but this is easily dismissed as soon as we give it any consideration at all. Does God have blue eyes or brown? Is he clean-shaven or bearded? Is he 5'10" or 6'4" tall? Above and beyond such simple anthropomorphisms has been the suggestion that we are created in the image of God in those areas of life whch can be defined as "spiritual." Men have self-consciousness, intellect, and will. They have creativity, and moral sense, and certain transcendental powers and positions above nature and judging it. Gloriously, we have the ability to enter into personal relationships with others of like inner structure—that is, we may have communion with God and with one another, and certain grand unities come into being as spirit touches spirit in friendship or in love.

Brunner's step beyond this is that the "image" of God, whatever it may be as a noun, can be understood better as a verb. Man is the image of God in the sense that he *images* God. God created man through the Word, so that, as Brunner states it, man is "being-in-the-Word," and so is a true man only in the fact of his constant response to the Word. This position, of course, needs some clarification. Man in his existence is dependent and contingent—man does not hold or have the power of existence in himself. (This is the wide field in which Tillich will stake out his claims.) Man's sin arises when in pride he believes that he can be the center of his own existence ("Ye shall be as gods"), or that he shall set his own standards ("knowing good from evil"). According to his own nature, he must depend on the existence which is grounded in the being of God, but in his rebellion he sets up his own center of operation and refuses to respond to God in obedience. This is his sin and it is also his destruction—this split, this schizo, this divided loyalty at the center.

As any amateur psychologist could point out, this sort of thing tears a man apart. This is disintegration, the dis-integer. Integer means "just one"; dis-integer means splitting the "one." Where there should be one center of life there are now two, and man literally disintegrates. The image of God, which is obedience to God or response to God, or the imaging of God's will, is now marred or destroyed—"You cannot serve God and mammon." Salvation, then, is to restore the image of God when we are led by faith to total commitment—"It is no longer I that live, but Christ liveth in me"; "For me to live is Christ." This new obedience is again the imaging of God. Christ, the model for man, said of Himself: "My meat and drink is to do the will of my Father." This was the sustenance of His life. This is how man is truly alive. Milton catches this perfectly in "Paradise Regained," where Christ fulfills all obedience "in the flesh."

With a little thought, one can see how all kinds of Christian thinking can have a new turn or a new interpretation from this insight of Brunner. Christianity is not an attainment, but a relationship. The "saints" of Corinth are live possibilities. As John Oman says: "It is not a question of the rung we occupy on the ladder; the question is whether we are climbing or falling." The "I-Thou" of Martin Buber is descriptive of our personal relationships; toward God this personal relationship is our image, our imaging. What this does to works, the earning of salvation, the traps of Phariseeism, the temptation to spiritual pride—all this is immediately evident, and eminently worth knowing.

We can give attention to *Dietrich Bonhoeffer* only briefly, and we consider him here, not so much because he has made a great contribution to theology (his total writings are very brief), but because young theologians, I feel, are reading what he has written and finding "in this martyr for a martyr faith" a call to high and noble dedication as they test their own theology in the pressures of life; as they show their faith by their works. In his two writings which can be classified as books—namely, *The Cost of Discipleship* and *Life Together*—we must draw out a theology which is not spelled out. It is evident that Bonhoeffer is truly in the Barthian tradition at the outset because of his use of the Bible. He accepts the Scriptures as they stand written as a body of canonical literature in which and through which the Word of God and the redemptive power of that Word are communicated. All is of God, all is of grace, and therefore man's only call is response; for he contributes nothing to his salvation except his own sin, and Bonhoeffer is in the Reformed tradition in his emphasis toward election.

Bonhoeffer's greatest contribution is in and around the general idea of "justification." He sets forth his beliefs in his book *The Cost of Discipleship*. For those who accept election and salvation by grace, justification by faith alone, there is always the temptation to lawlessness—*i.e.*, antinomianism. In Galatians, Paul has to battle for the faith at the crucial point of faith versus works. Significantly, after the doctrinal section of the letter as he turns to ethical application, he must battle the other side of the problem, the tendency toward antinomianism. How early and how easily this heresy arose. In Paul's letter to the Romans, we find him dueling with a questioner. Grace is a good thing, and the more sin, the more grace. Men should sin, therefore, so the reasoning goes, in order to increase grace. The question in Romans, therefore, is whether we should sin in order that grace may abound. Paul shouts it out: "God forbid!"

But, then, if a man does not work for his salvation (and this is the Romanist heresy and a temptation for all Protestants), then where is the place of good works? Paul said it, Augustine said it, the reformers said it, and Bonhoeffer had to say it again. He says it with his interesting phrase: "cheap grace." His contribution to modern theology is in his saying quite clearly again that we are made right by the righteousness of God, for there is nothing in us. Nevertheless, when we accept this free gift, the acceptance will be marked and verified by the works which follow. It is cheap grace indeed, we have cheapened grace—if we accept the salvation freely offered and then act as if nothing has happened. Works do not secure our salvation, but works follow our salvation; and a person who does not bring forth works "meet for repentance," has really never understood nor rightly accepted the grace of God in the first place—he has never entered the Father's house, the new environment of love and loving. In the true Reformed tradition, Bonhoeffer contributes a clear restatement of salvation by grace.

In *Reinhold Niebuhr* we have an expression of Barthian theology in ethics. Niebuhr began his ministry in the Bethel Evangelical Church of Detroit, where in the years 1915–28 he became increasingly distressed by what he judged to be the irrelevance of the Gospel in the social problems with which he was surrounded in that great industrial complex. What he had to say about the auto industry, particularly the effect of the assembly line on the total life of a man, caught the attention of a wide audience; in time, he was called to Union Seminary in New York City as professor of applied Christian ethics. In that chair and by way of writing and speaking, he continued in his self-assigned task of making Christianity ethically relevant. In the light of the so-called "social gospel" of the 1920's, and recognizing that in other ways Niebuhr is strongly on the side of the liberals, one is impressed by the fact that this man, who could be judged "liberal" in so many other ways, was like Karl Barth in two orthodox ways—first, in his recognition of the radical nature of sin; and second, in his use of the Bible as the center of Christian authority.

As in Barth, so in Niebuhr—we must be careful when we say that his approach is "Bible-centered." The acceptance of the Bible is the acceptance of the corpus, the body of writings. Whatever it is that God does with or through sacred writings, it will not be done outside of the canon of Scripture. What is done inside that canon of Scripture is where the differences between orthodoxy and neo-orthodoxy become drastically plain. The problem is not basically one of textual criticism, but of the various possible "higher" criticisms, plus the moot questions of hermeneutics. Is the third chapter of Genesis true, for example? Well, yes and no. How do you construe mythos? May not the Word in the midst of the words—namely, that man is a fallen creature—be the only matter of importance here? Or, with greater speculation, and this is Niebuhr himself beyond Barth, may this whole chapter not be best understood with a little psychologizing. Consider man's anxiety (his *angst*) as he tries to sustain the knife-edge of his humanity, sustained only in endless response to his Maker (this is Brunner's "image"). How easy to "fall," to choose the object of promise instead of just promise. So Niebuhr "uses" Scripture. Allowing for such treatment or mistreatment, it is only in the Bible that he finds the source, ground, and beginning of revealed truth.

The key to everything that Niebuhr has to say ethically lies in the title and in the thesis of one book, *Moral Man and Immoral Society*. This is not to evade his master work, the Gifford Lectures, *The Nature and Destiny of Man*. Those lectures, that book, is a different approach to the whole of his philosophy and surely establishes the foundation thinking for much that appears in his later writing. *Moral Man and Immoral Society* is an early work, is not a ponderous work, but is definitive of one controlling idea; when this idea is clearly understood, one has, it appears to me, the clue to Reinhold Niebuhr. What Niebuhr is saying is this. The moral man, however moral he may be, is touched with sin at the origin of every act, and is discolored with sin in the totality of his being. We mean here, of course, "original sin" and "total depravity," two old theological terms much shuddered at and seldom understood. "Original sin" means nothing about our being original in our sinning; sin is as old as Delilah or Jezebel and is not modern, sophisticated, or original. What it means is that at the origin of man there is sin, and that at the origin of every man there is sin. In every act, however good, there is discoloration in the origin. The discoloration is self-centeredness or pride. "Total depravity" does not mean that we are totally depraved; we are not utterly mad. But it does mean that the depravity of sin invades the totality of our persons, and so pervades all our social relationships.

Thus, moral man, the man of good will, brings to his every task his own built-in flaws. We are assuming here a man who wants to do the right thing and who has a high calling, not only to victory in his own life, but, by way of Christian compassion, to the alleviation of the problems of the world around him. When this man goes to work on the "immoral society" with which he is surrounded, it is not just a question of a good man against a sinful world, but it is a question of a sinner in a sinful world. Every good man brings his own problems to his own tasks, and his own problems can be very subtle. This is not a surrender to pessimism nor discouragement. It is a call to clear thinking about the nature of man and the nature of his predicament. In the last analysis, the moral man can do only two things: (1) He can choose the better action because the best action, the absolute, will never in this world of woe be a live option; (2) He can accept God's forgiveness for his sin and inadequacy and recognize that God will use what he has offered in his act and cover the rest, not with man's redemptive power, but with God's. In a year when we are having a presidential election we see exactly how the Niebuhr ethic works. A Christian as a Christian must vote. Not to vote is un-Christian to begin with. When he does vote, however, his action will be in no sense absolutely good. He will

40

cast his vote between two men, believing that one is better than the other. He will not be voting between good and bad, light and darkness, God and Satan. He will be voting for this sinner as against that sinner. In addition to this, he will bring to his choice all the ambiguities of the world situation, his best efforts to weigh a wide variety of values, and his efforts to weigh the sources of the information on which he will base his decision. And just what will the sources of information be? What guidelines will the news media and the trained commentators give him? We can accept that those who give us the news are limited men—limited in viewpoint and intelligence, not to speak of opportunities for careful, wise, and sober observation. Those who give us the news are limited human beings. Accepting this, we can suspect that they are not only limited but also slanted. They, too, may be moral men in immoral society; they may be immoral men in immoral society. Yet, based on their disclosures we must build our decisions, sometimes decisions for destiny.

William Temple, with his usual brilliance, having listened to Niebuhr at Swanwick, composed this wonderful limerick:

> At Swanwick when Niebuhr had quit it,
> Said a young theolog, now I've hit it!
> Since I cannot do right, I must find out tonight
> The right sin to commit and commit it.

This limerick is devasting, but still true. After the laughter has settled down one recognizes that what Temple is slyly prodding is exactly what Niebuhr himself wants most to say.

Our ethical choices have an absolute point of reference, but the choices themselves can never be absolute. This can be criticized as relativism in ethics, but it is not quite that. The touchstone for every decision is love—love for God and love for one's neighbor—so that in any existential situation each one of us is under the demands of God's kind of love. It is our Christian vocation, God's call. We make our decisions in penitence because we recognize that we are sinful men in a sinful society. "All our

41

righteousness is as filthy rags," but we make our decisions always in the direction of love. We recognize also that each man who is a servant of God owes allegiance to God, and not to anyone else. It is, therefore, quite possible that different men in what may seem to be the same situation may be called upon to do entirely different things for love's sake. Even more difficult is the fact that the same man may be called upon to do different things in what appear to be the same situations. This may look like inconsistency, but it can be sincere decision in sober truth.

A simple illustration is in the methods of a parent toward a recalcitrant child. Who is wise enough for such things? For love's sake he might well discipline with some harshness in a given week of rebellion and decide on the fifth day to try something entirely different. Perhaps, for example, one should never use corporal punishment on a child with an institutional background. By the same token, perhaps one ought to spank his own child, who knows himself surrounded by a household of love. We recognize that we do operate according to the insights which Niebuhr has organized for us, even though we back away from what appears to be highly subjective, unstructured, inconsistency as principle. His whole system is shot through with what we have already discussed in the intellectual background of modern theology and it illustrates especially the nonpropositional, loosely defined theology of Barth. We have in Reinhold Niebuhr relativism in action, based on an absolute foundation. Not everyone can carry this kind of anxiety, awaiting decision—we want black and white, the absolute decision, now. As Barth would say, we live in crisis. We walk by faith: "one step enough."

4

Bultmann and Tillich

IT IS NOT necessary to approach *Rudolf Bultmann* by way of apology, although it is necessary to approach him by way of explanation. All of us, it seems to me, are facing the same problem in modern theology. The mass of original material is tremendous, and the commentaries on these originals multiply daily. A review of a book by Arnold Come some months ago quoted him as saying that he had worked his way through Barth's *Dogmatik* as a daily assignment, and that in so doing he had worked 10 to 12 hours a day for a whole academic year. It is this sort of assignment that any honest man has when he faces, not only Barth, but Brunner, Niebuhr, Bultmann, Tillich, and all those others who are beginning to find their places on the secondary levels of modern theology. One approaches a man like Bultmann, therefore, recognizing the impossibility of complete coverage, even if one can assume for himself complete understanding; one is troubled even to find a proper vantage point from which to view him. All this is by way of explanation, not apology.

Bultmann is a modern theologian in the old liberal tradition, picking up where German rationalism had left off before the impact of Karl Barth. He is the latest thrust of the old form-criticism in the study of the Gospels, and his use of the method is complete and some think completely disintegrating. He has no hesitance in bringing to bear on every Biblical writing every critical device. He can accept where he wishes and discard as he pleases. He can introduce a wide range of manuscripts and authorities. He can discover influences, whether Gnostic or Hellenistic. He does all this quite freely and frankly and in all candor. He does it sometimes without any visible means of support. Consider one illustration from his *Theology of the New Testament* (vol. I, p. 148): ". . . and it is in this direction that Mark cast his account of the Last Supper in the form of an etiological cultnarrative by working the eucharistic liturgy into an older traditional account which reported the Last Supper as a Passover meal." This is typical also: ". . . 'for I received of the Lord'—is not appeal to a personal revelation from the Lord although this is frequently assumed, but it is a tradition handed down to him being ultimately derived from the Lord" (vol. I, p. 150). In this sort of statement Bultmann does not think that it is incumbent on him to give us any proof or support, and his works are full of this sort of treatment. One feels increasingly that his is an attitude of condescension toward the rest of us, who can't quite see (a) whether all this be true, and (b) just how Bultmann is qualified to say so.

One reads Bultmann's *Theology of the New Testament* with increasing irritation if one, early in the reading, takes any notice of assumptions and presuppositions. One would be a very busy fellow peeling these all away. In the tradition where Bultmann is at home, certain things are assumed by him which might still be highly debatable: the dating of the Gospels; the validity of John as a basic source; the reality of such things as Q, Ur-Mark, *ta loggia;* the question as to the origins of ideas, whether in the Scriptures toward the ancient world or in the ancient world toward the Scriptures. Bultmann's theology is a rather recent one, but more recently, particularly by way of archaeology and particularly by way of the Dead Sea scrolls, it is being seen by those who are willing to read with some honesty outside of the liberal tradition, that what "everybody knows," everybody doesn't really know. New Testament studies are in great new flux, and the flow seems to be in the direction of orthodoxy. The "assured findings" of modern scholarship are gaining a different kind of assurance, in spite of which Bultmann is still treating the New Testament in the same old way.

Interestingly enough, Bultmann in his criticisms is not afraid of "other wordliness" nor of the supernatural. Indeed, he glories in it. This denies, of course, one of the easy criticisms of the liberal—that he refuses the miraculous and then from such a position easily rationalizes his rationalistic positions. This is not true of Bultmann, as it is clearly not true of Barth. In the realities of the things of the Spirit, Bultmann never wavers. He speaks plainly, and I think with excitement, of the "reign of God" which breaks in with Christ. His approach to New Testament theology is, not only radical, but eschatological.

At the same time, and this is interesting when one feels that Bultmann abuses Scripture, his writing is chained to Scripture; most of his disciples and followers insist that all he has to say is a Biblical theology. In a sense this is true, once Bultmann can decide what constitutes the Bible. Whereas many have undertaken to write their own Bibles, from Strauss to Thomas Jefferson, Bultmann's approach has its own flavor. For reasons of demythologizing (which we shall shortly treat), he virtually dismisses the synoptic Gospels as sources for his theology. He then must reduce the writings of Paul by accepting easily (much too easily) most of the arguments against Pauline authorship. With a small sheaf of manuscripts which he can accept as Pauline, he finally has the groundwork for his theology in the "writings" of Paul. The rest of his theology centers around what he is willing to call the "Johannine literature." In and around all this is his readiness to see Gnosticism and Hellenism under every verb. Yes, he is a Biblical theologian, but only when he decides what constitutes the Bible. For the general reader the writings of Bultmann can, in a limited way, be helpful, for they are rich and profound in exegetical insights, and I know of no man who is more objective and helpful when he turns aside for individual word studies.

Just how may one characterize what is central and definitive in

Bultmann's theology? It is the word "demythologize" which comes immediately to mind. Loetscher in the *Twentieth Century Encyclopedia* makes the following statement in regard to both Bultmann and Dibelius: "Christianity created myths of its own around the historical facts, especially countless legends surrounding baptism and the Eucharist, and the myth of the descent of the heavenly redeemer as applied to Jesus." According to Bultmann, the purpose of the Gospel message was never to *describe* supernatural events taking place in space and time, but rather was intended to announce God's coming into man's soul and the radical change thus accomplished. The whole redemption event is completed existentially in the believer and need not be located in any other history than in that personal history.

Perhaps this can be made clearer if we understand that the early church knew and testified, because of what happened to them personally, that there was a core of truth or kerygma concerning Jesus of Nazareth, and they built around this core of truth what we find in the Gospels—a "Gospel story." In the first century the problem of the early church was to put the "Gospel story" in the language and the thought forms acceptable to that day, and they, therefore, created such myths as the virgin birth, the wise men, the miracles, the resurrection, the transfiguration, and the ascension in order to make the wonder of what had happened to them understandable to the people of their day. One is reminded of the wisdom of John Baillie's remark that, believing in God, we set about proving the existence of God to others because we already believe that He does exist. If the belief in God came to us personally a priori by experience, why do we hope to make a believer out of another man a posteriori by proof?

How, then, did the unbelievers in the early church believe in the resurrection apart from a resurrection (Markus Barth is excellent on this in his *Acquittal by Resurrection*), and were they being forced to invent a different ground of belief for the sake of their hearers than the ground on which they became believers in the first place?

Bultmann insists that the early church was not denying that God had broken into life in a unique way in Jesus of Nazareth, and they were not denying, according to Bultmann, that there was such a Person and that He was in some sense the revelation of God. They were not denying that, in the early church, members of that church had had a Christian experience, and that in each case a believer could be sure that the living Christ was alive in him. What Bultmann is denying for the early church is th t they really believed the "forms" of the Gospels with which they surrounded the core of the Gospels. If Bultmann is correct, then within fifty years of Christ's birth, those committed to the C ne who called Himself the "Truth," those who would in many cases die for the Truth, such ones invented the virgin birth, the miracles, the transfiguration, the resurrection, and the ascension, better to convince others of the Truth. The early church, apparently, was busy erecting a construction around Jesus of Nazareth to make Him look like what God ought to look like in the first century when He came on the human scene.

The problem of "demythologizing" is to strip away what in Bultmann's judgment is inescapably first-century myth in order to find that basic core of truth. The next step is to "remythologize" by making out of this core material our twentieth-century mythos by using the language and thought modes of our own day. In our day, we can dismiss demons in terms of depth psychiatry. Miracles are no longer aids to belief, but stumbling blocks, and, therefore, should be discarded. The bodily resurrection must be subjected to the analysis of matter by modern physicists, and some of the space imagery, such as the ascension, must be transferred from the God "out there" or the God "up there" to the God (and I mean *Honest to God*) who is not really "down there," but who is still the ground of our being. When this is done, it is held that the modern man finds the whole Gospel thing quite acceptable and can now, when he could not before (is this true of all twentieth-century converts?), experience in his own life existentially and personally the incarnation of Christ. In this marvelous way, Bultmann would maintain, the whole Gospel can come alive in our new day. What broke into the first century is to break in now. It is not a question of what Jesus *said*, but what He now *says;* it is not a question of what He *did*, but what He now *does*.

However much there is acceptable in Bultmann, we must register at least one strong criticism before we leave him. We are glad that he is in some sense a Biblical theologian, because so long as we stay in the context of the Bible there is hope for all of us; God's Word can yet break through in surprising ways. We are highly appreciative of the lavishness of his scholarship. We are not unhappy about his emphasis on the living Christ *in us now*, and we think we need the emphasis. We must recognize afresh, and Bultmann helps us here, that we are to be "epistles known and read of men." We are in some sense an extension of the incarnation; the church is the Body of Christ. The living Word ought to be alive in us.

What is so puzzling about Bultmann, and others like him, is just how it is that they know what Christianity is all about, or what constitutes its core, or just what it is about Christ that ought to come alive in us, when they keep picking to pieces the only records we have, the only witness available to the very thing which they insist is so precious. How do they know, for example, that our personal Christian reactions in 1966 ought to be wholly "in love," or that the church in our day ought to manifest the community of love, unless somewhere they have laid their hands on an authoritative word. Sometimes it seems like circular reasoning. That God is love, and that we are saved by grace, is apparent from Luke to Ephesians. Having found this teaching a warm and happy and encouraging one, it is easy to make of this the clue to, and perhaps finally the judge of, the Scriptures. What is not of love, then becomes suspect. The idea of love can, at the same time, step away from the holy-love of a P.T. Forsythe to the sentimental love of the jukebox. In any case, what does not conform to this "love" motif is not essential Gospel, so dismiss the rest. The conclusion, then, with the non-love elements excluded, is that the Gospels speak to us of nothing but love.

If they will not accept the words of Scripture as they stand, what do they offer us for our common understanding and accept- ance. It is one thing for a German and a German-trained theolo- gian to gallop off in all directions as far and as fast as he likes with his subtleties and his speculations. Whether this is good methodology for leading a flock is something else again. This stuff may be good stuff for theological debating. What it will look like when it seeps down into a teaching quarterly for young people is something else again. Think for a moment of the fol- lowing statement, which appeared in a Protestant teaching pub- lication a couple of years ago. It is pure Bultmann. It is a state- ment regarding Jesus' raising of Lazarus from the dead (and I paraphrase): "We are not supposed to believe that Jesus raised Lazarus from the dead. This story was put in here merely to assure us that Jesus has the power of life and death." One is left on dead-center with writing like that. It is frustrating to discover how to face it. If Jesus had the power of life and death, was there any real problem to His raising Lazarus? Would there have been a better way to assure us of that power beyond His actually performing such a miracle? Should our confidence rest better in that act of Jesus or in a feeling of assurance in the early church? In any case, where does the easy assurance of the commentator on this Lazarus incident arise? One suspects he trusts Bultmann more than John (why?) and passes this on to the readers of church-school quarterlies, without even suggesting that some other viewpoint might have merit, and that his own viewpoint very recent and very debatable.

My basic criticism of Bultmann is perhaps best stated and b started by Giovanni Miegge in *Gospel and Myth in the Thou* of *Roudolf Bultmann:* "The more Jesus' incalculable unique and overpowering creativity are removed from the figure of J in the gospels, the more they have to be attributed instead to Christian community." Bultmann is quite wary of positiv spiration in the New Testament records; meanwhile, he a ently accepts quite easily the inspiration of the early chur which the Gospels and epistles are written. But even the

church had no starting place apart from the original and basic Gospel sources. The shift of the story from the Gospel records to the inspiration of the Christians of the early church creates Bultmann's own little myth. He wants us to believe the unbelievable miracle that people like us could have created a figure like Christ. Horace Bushnell in famous chapter X of his *Nature and the Supernatural* gives virtually the final answer to any idea of the matchless Christ figure—both life and teaching—as being an invention or creation by anyone. Fairbairn turns aside in his *Philosophy of the Christian Religion* to show in a different way the impossibility of the idea that the followers of Christ invented or created. As against Bultmann, Bushnell emphasizes that to create the Person of Christ would have been a miracle of psychological understanding; Fairbairn sees it as a miracle of art. Only the simple, sincere, serene confidence of eyewitnesses could have brought the whole thing off. And the teaching also—if the teaching of Jesus is not authentically Jesus' teaching, we are faced with the amazing fact that ordinary people dreamed it all up. Bultmann strains on a gnat and swallows a camel.

Paul Tillich was a theological "loner," more a philosopher than a theologian, exploring the deeps where sometimes his disciples could go with him, but where more often they get lost. How can one put his finger on the core and center of this man's work?

At the age of 47 he had already made his impact on theology, but began life anew in the United States first at Union Theological Seminary in New York and then preeminently as a "university professor" at Harvard. As a university professor (not a professor in the university), he was to reach out as a theologian and touch on other faculties and disciplines. This assignment helps to explain his theology. Tillich was reaching out for that far point in Christian theology where it is most likely to touch and challenge any other area of thought—physics, sociology, and especially philosophy—where the claims of Christianity are not acceptable and where the dominant belief is unbelief. Is there

anything that can be said about God as "Being in general" before we say anything specific about Jesus Christ, or about the preaching of the church, or even about a church picnic, which the man or woman offended by Christianity must accept as a starting point? If this point can be stated, is it possible to lead such a "believer in general," step by step, to what might be called a "full-orbed Gospel"? This, possibly, is whatever Evangel Tillich would have to offer. Out there in the misty flats of philosophy, Tillich's approach may give an unbeliever a prod in the right directions. Meanwhile, scores of divinity students draw such comfort as they can from having such a "champion" representing them in the arena of Academe.

Sometimes when we give the devil his due, we give him too much due. Sometimes, in trying to reach the world where it is, we sacrifice too much of that which is unique and demanding in our own faith. It is because of such possibilities that Tillich is wide open to the criticism of Christians of a wide variety of confessions. People who don't understand Tillich cannot see how he is Christian at all, and people who understand him best are not always sure that they want to follow him as far as he goes, and many of them feel that he gives too much to the "enemy." Consider that such a man as Nels Ferre, writing in *Christendom* (1948), refers to Tillich's *The Protestant Era* as a book which ". . . overflows with creative insights and sound practical counsels. It is . . . provocative of new orientations. In numerous instances . . . Tillich reveals authentic scientific powers. . . . If such a person and thinker would only become more centered on the bed rock of Biblical faith, he could use even more completely his concern for and outreach toward the secular world and his theology would have more steadiness and life for a confused and wistful church." As James Luther Adams says: "Mystery becomes more important than meaning; myth more important than doctrine." Perhaps a too harsh criticism, although a delightful one, comes from James Hastings Nichols in *The Christian Century* (July 14, 1948): "If it were not for Tillich's own general introduction somehow autobiographical in character . . . you might recommend that this book be read backwards."

What is most distinctive in Tillich's philosophic theology and that which takes him to the far reaches of human thought is his effort to talk about "being" as over against "non-being." Most readers are not accustomed to this kind of language and do not use it easily. When *Time Magazine* featured Tillich and even called him "Mr. Protestant," a great many people, especially Protestants, were amazed to read the catch quotation on the *Time* cover, allegedly Tillich's words: "God does not exist." This was hard for Protestants to take from "Mr. Protestant."

We recognize the problem of semantics, of course, and we are always expecting special language problems in German theologians and philosophers. According to Tillich, God is "Being" itself, or "the Power of Being whereby it resists non-being." He is the "Is-ness" or, as God spoke to Moses at the burning bush, He is the "I am that I am," the ever always present tense of the verb "to be." Men have existence. Animals have existence. The world has existence, but God is the ground of Being out of which all existence can arise or within which all existence is possible. Men and animals can cease to exist. In such use of the term, God does not exist, and He does not have existence. He is the Being on which all existence depends.

This kind of language sounds "way out" because it is, but out there perhaps Tillich can get a physicist, a philosopher, or maybe even a sociologist or psychiatrist, to admit that the one thing inescapable, even in an argument where we are trying to deny everything, is the ground of being where we take our stand in order to argue at all. As we all well know, discussion can't move without some presuppositions, some "givens," general acceptances. What Tillich is maintaining as a starting place, and he sounds like another rationalist—Descartes, with his *cogito ergo sum*—is the inescapable datum, necessarily accepted as a starting place: Being as over against non-being. God is this Being. As Descartes could start from one statement and move on to substance and God, Tillich makes the same attempt and with some success. He is more successful as a Theist than as a Christian, and as an evangelical Christian he is not successful at all.

Since God is Being (all there is of Being) then whatever man is, will of necessity be related to, be dependent on, that only basic Reality. Men are wholly dependent, contingent. Our "courage to be" is an acceptance in faith of this existence of ours as wholly dependent (think again here of Niebuhr's *angst*). One rests in the Lord. At any moment a man can go out like a light; just to think of this fact steadily for a few moments is distressing, maybe even disheartening. The fact remains. But if we are to live, then let us live positively and victoriously. It was Jesus Christ who had preeminently this courage to be. He shows us how such an obedient and faithful life is lived—"my meat and drink is to do the will of my Father"—and we have our "imitation of Christ." Since, however, He participates in our humanity, His victorious life may be a union with our life; He not only gives us the example, but gives us of His life. He is Lord—and Saviour.

With regard to the actual historical Jesus, we must recognize that Tillich accepts the incarnation as having happened, and he assures us that the Biblical picture of Jesus is the picture of Jesus as the Christ. He accepts the Gospel Jesus as an object of historical inquiry, but only as having a high degree of probability, and he seems to be a little stronger than Bultmann in maintaining that the kind of person Jesus was supports the Biblical picture of Him. The Christian participates in the incarnation "partly as a member of a church . . . and partly as an individual grasped by the revealing event and becoming contemporaneous with it."

The "crisis" in Barth, the "imaging" of God in Brunner, the existential ethical choice in Niebuhr, these find expression again in Tillich. Every moment of every day, a man walks in utter dependence, obeying as the Word siezes him. His "courage to be" is this daily dependence, and the issues are in God's hands. A man doesn't have to know much to live like this, and he can't know very many things for sure, which makes one wonder about the quantity of information Tillich thinks we need in his three-volume theology, not to speak of his ethical works!

Tillich's theology becomes revealed best in the arena of life, and one feels that he walks more freely in this ethical material than in his philosophical theology, although it may be because this material lies closer to our understanding. In the predicament of our existence, and in the tussle of our days, and in the ambiguities of our decisions, Tillich sees God in Christ reaching out toward us. Our sin is not rebellion against our Maker, so much as a refusal to respond to Him and to receive what He has for us. God has an answer for our human predicament, and, in treating of this answer, Tillich is at his best. Here one could wish it possible to expand in this brief treatment the richness of Tillich's thought. The limitations of human rationality are met by God's revelation. Our finitude finds answer in the Being of God. Human sin finds answer in Christ. The need for man's living unity or community is answered by the Holy Spirit, and our anxieties about destiny are answered in the Kingdom of God.

All this attempts to pick up human doubt and anxiety, wherever man finds himself in his human predicament, to bring him back to God. It is not to be expected that we shall find the old theological language or the old thought modes in Tillich. He has his own standpoint and viewpoint. All his writings hold to a system for "Being" in God and the promise of fullness of life in us. One gathers from Tillich's writings that he is not really difficult once one gets his slant; one feels, however, that of all the contemporary theologians, Tillich's writings will have the hardest time sustaining themselves, except in esoteric groups.

5

Counter-Thrust

SOMETIMES TO OVERSIMPLIFY is to falsify, and, as we have tried to say more than once, in addition to the problem of making modern theology clear, there is the more basic problem of the mass of material from which some pattern of thought can be drawn and from which certain conclusions may be made valid.

It seems to me, nevertheless, that from the past fifty years in theology, with the emphasis that has been thrown on the side of neo-orthodoxy and liberalism, certain things are clear, certain gifts of the whole movement are evident and are to be noted. And we suggest these before turning to some criticisms.

The first gift comes under the general heading of "Biblical theology." Even a man like Bultmann can be called a Biblical theologian, and we must recognize that the neo-orthodox movement and even the new liberalism continue to center in and on the *textus receptus*. We can argue the destructiveness of the critical apparatus, but we also carry with us a measure of faith and hope that there is nothing to bring a man back to the truth quite like a close study of the Scriptures. Even young graduates of theological seminaries, steeped in Barth and Bultmann, have already begun to shift towards orthodoxy because they have been taught to work in and at the Scriptures. Coupled with this Biblical theology there must be recognition of serious and meticulous scholarship; and, if the impact of modern theology is to be met, it cannot be met with anything less than the same careful work.

One sees in modern theology a heightening of subjective faith, which is another way of saying that there is a new emphasis on religious "experience." This is strange, in a way, but we do discover that one of the end products in modern, liberal theology is that a man often experiences in his faith something similar to that found in a campfire meeting or "tent" evangelism gathering. This, of course, has been true since the days of Schleiermacher, when, in the liberal tradition, "feeling" was made the clue to Christianity. I am quite sure that Bultmann and one of the current, favorite song leaders would not appreciate each other's company, but the fact remains that both of them would probably be working on feeling in religion as opposed to reasoning or, more accurately, subjective experience as against a sturdy rationale.

It is impossible to escape the Christocentric quality of modern theology. Barth is never better than when he is discussing Christ and his redemptive power. Bultmann, while playing down the possibility of any picture of the historical Jesus, nevertheless makes the Christ of the "creeds" the essence of our faith; and Tillich in his doctrines journeys from the Being of God to the problems of the day and makes Christ the clue. Perhaps our superficial training in philosophy, which is characteristic of most education in America, is what makes it most difficult for us to understand why it is that German theologians have to say such simple things in such complex ways, and yet, however subtle may be their approach, they are witnessing constantly to the inescapable Christ.

One common note among modern theologians is their basic call to action in love. Here again, we may find our spirits resisting them in what looks like an overemphasis on love as against holiness or righteousness, or an emphasis on love that seems sometimes to dismiss the very rectitude of God. It is the other end of the spectrum from legalistic moralisms and the dangers of Phariseeism. Well, who can escape the suspicion within himself that he may become hard and legalistic. Even if we look upon the emphasis on love as an imbalance, we have to recognize the necessity of its constant criticism of hard legalism. Men naturally prefer decisions in black and white and absolute values of good and bad, but this could be the mark of a sophomore mind. The general indefiniteness of this modern approach to ethics brings out another gift of modern theology—namely, its dynamic openness. It can be chilly and frightening when one breaks away from theological and ethical fixed points, and not many want to move in this direction of freedom; the percentage of losses can be very high. We can wish also for a little more manifestation of stability and some concern for the conservation of old findings, but this characteristic, open-ended love motif, with all its crises is, in my opinion, one of the greatest, most significant gifts of modern theology; it can lead to greatness.

Some criticisms seem now in order. The first criticism is a very old one—namely, the disintegrating effect of the radical criticism of Scriptures, not so dangerous for the world of Biblical scholarship, as in the mind and heart of the simple Bible reader. Except in some few instances, I can see no way at all that the layman can become trained in the apparatus which lies behind the literary criticism of the Old and New Testaments. Even after three years in a theological seminary, unless the student has a certain flair for this sort of thing, he is lost in confusion, and the man who has the flair is not really fitted for critical tasks until he has had many, many years of scholarly training far beyond the three years of seminary. Assuming that "the assured findings of scholarship" are in any sense still debatable among the scholars, and I for one think they are constantly so, how can a seminary student be equipped to argue the case, with one year of Hebrew and one year of Greek, and how shall the layman judge these matters, with no formal training beyond his college days, if he went to college, plus a few summer conferences or lay retreats, where he has probably been given big shots of churchmanship and not even a taste of scholarship. This sounds like obscurantism, but it is not. It is not a plea for ignorance nor for the folding up of our tents of scholarship.

The experience of my own denomination would indicate, however, that two things might be done. Firstly, highly debatable matters fed to our people by way of curriculum, for example, might be marked as highly debatable, and an opportunity might be given for the other side of the debate to be heard. Even though a statement may be true, the introduction to the statement with some such rubric as "everybody knows" or "scholars agree" makes me immediately nervous. It is like reading in the minutes that a man has been given a vote of confidence. Generally, this means that some kind of lack of confidence necessitated the vote of confidence! In any case, the end of the matter has been that the kind of people who used to feed daily on the Word of God no longer do so because there is a general suspicion that the Book in their hands is no longer trustworthy. This means that when the theological styles have changed again and Bultmann is given no more attention, say, than Anselm, the great mass of Bible-believing Christians, around which another new theology might grow, or from whom students for our theological seminaries might continue to come, will have been diluted away.

Secondly, in my own theological lifetime it seems to me that one of the greatest shifts has been away from inspiration to revelation. It is hard to get modern theologians to talk about the inspired Bible. In Barth, the revelatory word includes everything from that which is written to the resultant action, and inspiration does not lie in the creation of the Bible, but in the act of the Spirit on the Word of the Bible in the action of the believer. Authority shifts from the inception of the Word—"it stands written"—to the action of the believer, and, however much we may want to encourage action, we must recognize that the Word of God stands secure, whether we ever act on it or not. It does stand written, and hopefully this could lead to our action, but it may also stand written as judgment against us. Its truth does not depend on us. As H. L. Tomlinson said in *Out of Soundings:* "What a man cannot see may condemn him." It may condemn *him*. It can be all the worse for me, not for the Word of God, that it doesn't particularly appeal to me right now in my existential situation.

What is meant really by all this emphasis on the mighty acts of God? The Bible becomes a record of the mighty acts of God in a certain contemporary situation. The Bible is not a record of the truth, but a record of what men thought about the truth. There is a real division here between orthodox theology and the new theology. No one denies that the great acts of God took place—the crossing of the Red Sea, the fall of Samaria, the fall of Jerusalem, the captivity, the coming of Christ. What orthodox theology must insist on is that "men moved by the Holy Spirit spoke from God." Not only are the acts of God revelatory, but God inspired His men to speak a word of interpretation *on* and *about* these acts. This is a real cleavage, and orthodox theology must continue to hold to inspiration as much as to revelation.

Reason and natural theology, another area of debate, are perhaps interrelated, for, of course, our reasoning power is one of our natural gifts, and men in every nation and clime have sought God with their minds. Even with a revelation from God, there are reasons for faith. The debate between reason and faith reached its climax in the medieval church and is not yet downed, and I know of no theologian who has completely mastered the interrelation between these two; but the reality of the faith experience must not blind us to the other gift of God, the powers of reasoning faculties, nor must we evade the responsibility for their good use. One cannot expect to enclose the infinite God in the finite mind or to limit God by definition, but to suppose that we can have a body without bones in it, or take a journey without the acceptance of a map, or establish a theology without definition or system is to urge nonsense. One does not fall in love with a bag of bones or a hank of hair, but one shudders over a boneless, hairless possibility. The pudding-face appearance of much of religion in our day is crying out for the bones of definitive, propositional theology.

One other criticism is that whatever can be said in favor of the critical importance of the existential moment must not blind us to absolutes and authorities. What can one say at the side of a deathbed, for example, regarding our future hope? If we do not believe what Jesus said, or even question whether He said it at all, then what is there for us to say to someone who wants to *know*. I think there are great advantages in decisions in love in the existential situation, but just how can a pastor explain to a dying man that belief in the next world is existential? Whatever happens in the next world cannot possibly build on any existential moment in this world. "Let not your heart be troubled," and why not? Because you believe that there will come to pass that which has been promised, but such promises lie in the future and in the eternal order, rather than in the temporal, and nothing vaguely resembling the existential moment has any bearing whatsoever.

There is a countermovement, as we know, in the orthodox tradition. Some even think it may have a name, called "neo-fundamentalism," but, unless it was picked just for the fun of it or to be in the theological swim of things, the name has very little to recommend it. Men like Henry, Carnell, Clark, Ramm, and Gerstner, not to speak of preachers like Graham, have nothing "neo" about them. There has, instead, been a stubborn refusal by many to leave the old orthodoxy and a reasoned theology, and there has been with them no foundation for scholarly embarrassment or apology in maintaining the orthodox tradition.

In addition to individual efforts, publications like *Christianity Today,* and the several publications of the Graham Foundation, and the refurbishment of many of the publishers of Bible-school curricula have been sources of new strength. Westminster and Fuller Seminaries have maintained high levels of scholarship with a devotion to the essence of the faith. Wheaton College, with no apology for academic excellence, stands high also in its concern for the faith. Bible colleges are a phenomena of our day and are an answer in many different ways to the neglect of the Bible in most educational institutions. Such movements as Young Life or Intervarsity Fellowship have generated new commitment in high schools and in college communities. Christian Businessmen and variations of this in law, medicine, and the like, have given opportunity to many people who have worried about the trends and tendencies of their old-line denominations. Lay movements of all sorts, with a deep seriousness and a fine simplicity of approach, have been springing up all over the country; and, if one believes in prayer at all, the phenomenal multiplication of prayer groups will give opportunity in God's time for God's breakthrough.

What are some of the characteristics of these countermovements? First, in season and out of season, and in spite of confusions and alarms, there is the constancy of effort for the maintenance and thrust of the historical faith; the Biblical record is inspired and trustworthy, and the loyalty for and to the words of Scripture is maintained. What light is yet to break out of the Word of God one cannot say, but there is a recognition that there is always a plus-factor in the Scripture—we feed upon the Word of God and absorb many things beyond what we know ourselves—and this plus-factor is evident to anyone who will accept the Bible on its own claims.

This historical faith can be given definition and grander statement in reasonable terms which men of like reason can find acceptable. No one says now, and I don't think anyone ever really did say, that everything can be said of God in human speech. We do not expect to have "God in a box." But we can say certain things that are true, which means that certain other things are not true, or, more exactly, that certain things *go,* which is in opposition to the attitude that *anything goes.*

In a day given over to the easy acceptance of church union, or in some cases a devotion and commitment to the principle of union, there is another union not quite in tune with the publicized sweep of things, an ecumenical movement centered around an appreciation of the authority of Scripture, the use of creeds, and the acceptance of denominational identity. In an ecclesiastical atmosphere where it is almost impossible to get your fellow churchmen to say what it is that defines your own denomination theologically (let us all be Christians, not Baptists or Presbyterians), this very refusal to draw lines because they make divisions, is an offense to Truth, which is by its nature divisive. More than that, the attitude of mind which evades theological niceties in denominational affairs is the same cast of mind which will not draw the lines in ethics. For those who tell me not to be a legalist, I can only answer: "Do you want me to be an illegalist?" The law stands, and the ethic of love is not to be a denial of the law, but the heart of the law and the positive possibilities beyond the law. I do not become illegal or immoral for love's sake, but I become legal and moral for love's sake and then go beyond the law in grace.

The same cast of mind can well mean that we will blur the distinctions between Protestantism and Catholicism "for the sake of unity," and we are not too far away from the day when there will be those in high places who will be recommending again the breaking of the lines between Christianity and Buddhism, an appeal for an eclecticism with something for everybody.

The countermovement in theology today is committed to giving meticulous and sharp study to the words of Scripture, the definitions of theology, the absolutes of ethics, and the differentia of the churches.